THEY DID IT!

ROHIT SHARMA

RED
PANDA

First published by Red Panda, an imprint of Westland Publications Private Limited, in 2020

1st Floor, A Block, East Wing, Plot No. 40, SP Infocity, Dr MGR Salai, Perungudi, Kandanchavadi, Chennai 600096

The content, facts, events and statements contained in this book have been compiled from publicly available documents and are not intended to defame anyone or infringe upon any person's privacy. The authors have made every effort to ensure the accuracy and veracity of the contents in this book. The authors and publisher do not assume and expressly disclaim any liability to any person (natural or legal) for any losses or damages caused by errors or omissions.

ISBN: 9789389648133
10 9 8 7 6 5 4 3 2 1

Content and book design by Write Media
All images have been sourced from IANS

Printed at Aarvee Promotions

Contents

Unstoppable Rohit

Rohit Sharma is a batting powerhouse. He is the only cricketer to have scored THREE double hundreds in One-Day Internationals (ODIs). He is a player with elegance and class. Rohit's unique talent and grip over his attacking shots make him stand out from other players.

This 33-year-old opening batsman's rock-solid presence on the 22 yards inspires not just his fans but Team India as well. As long as he is batting, India always has a good chance of winning the match. With several international and Indian cricketing records under his belt, Rohit is already one of the greatest batsmen in the history of ODIs.

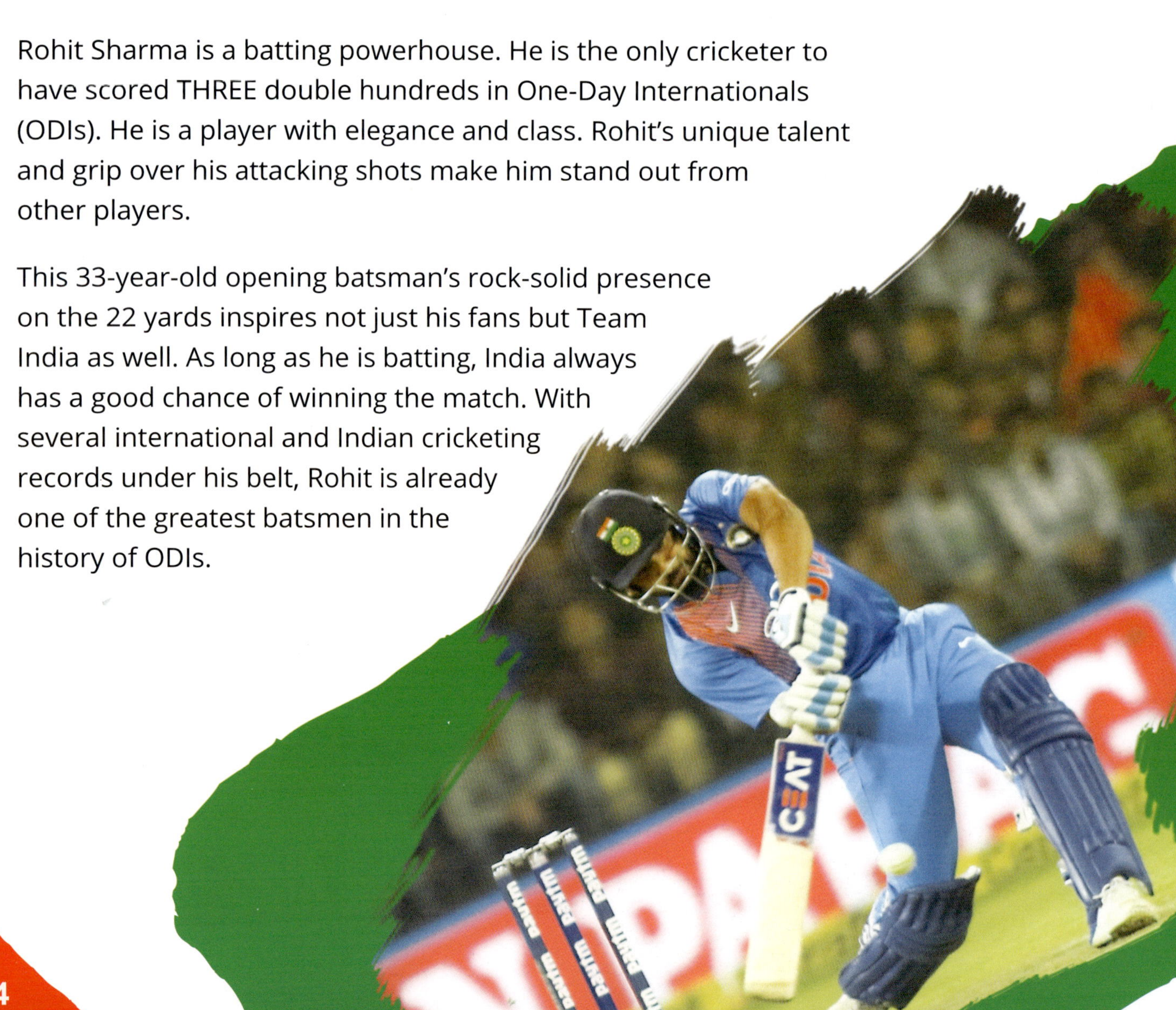

‘It pumps me up—the whole idea of the bowler marking his run-up, popping at the crease, the crowd chanting, nerves building up. It’s a very good feeling. Right from the first ball, I know I have to be at the top of my game.’

It's the Moment that Matters

At first, Rohit Sharma comes across as the quintessential boy next door, and perhaps not the power batsman that India boasts of today. When he strides on to the field and towards the pitch, his walk is relaxed and his face expressionless. But the moment the bowler runs down the crease and raises his arm to bowl, Rohit's eyes widen, and there is a determined look on his face. His focus is on the ball coming towards him. You can almost read his thoughts, 'I have to hit it hard and far ...'

Did you know?

Like most parents, Rohit's mother wanted him to study hard and get a good job. She did not want him to be a cricketer. But, Rohit had his eyes set on the sport. He followed his dream and the rest, as they say, is history.

He is fantastic. Rohit is poetry in motion because the kind of bat swing he has, not many players possess. A class apart when it comes to the smooth swing. You could see the effort put in, when he hit that six, was minimal. A number of guys have multiple bat swings but not a clean swing. Rohit's swing is like a pendulum.

~ Sachin Tendulkar
at the 2019 World Cup

The Twists and Turns

Rohit Gurunath Sharma was born on 30 April 1987 in Nagpur, Maharashtra, to Purnima and Gurunath Sharma. His father worked as a caretaker in a transport company and his mother is a homemaker. Rohit has a younger brother named Vishal.

When Rohit was a toddler, his family shifted to a small house in Dombivali, a suburb in Mumbai, to save on expenses. Rohit was sent to live with his grandparents and uncles in nearby Borivali. He usually met his parents only on weekends.

Rohit the Dreamer

Rohit began showing interest in cricket at the age of eight. He dreamt of playing for India. He would play for hours on end and then discuss every shot in detail with his family, who are all keen cricket enthusiasts.

Passion and Talent

Rohit has a large extended family. All his six uncles are sports lovers and played cricket for their respective schools and colleges.

Enthusiasm, combined with an analysis of the game, seemed like just the right mix for young Rohit. The elders in the family could see the spark and were keen to encourage him. So they all got together and decided to help him join a cricket academy in 1999. This was a stepping stone to bigger things.

Later, Dinesh Lad, the coach at the academy, insisted that Rohit leave his school, Our Lady of Vailankanni High School, and join Swami Vivekananda International School, which boasted of better cricket training facilities. Aware of his family's financial constraints, Rohit was not too keen to attend the new school as it was expensive. But Dinesh came to his rescue and managed to arrange a scholarship for him, exempting Rohit from paying the school fees for the next four years. This was the beginning of the rise of Rohit Sharma.

Rohit has got all the shots to be a Virender Sehwag. He has been dynamic.

~ Graeme Smith

Master of the Bat

He's a special batsman. The beauty of Rohit is that he plays effortlessly.

~ Pravin Amre

Rohit worked hard at his training even though he was often late for his practice sessions. He had explained to the coach that it was not easy for him to get to the field on time every day since he slept in the living room and was unable to sleep until the television was switched off by the others. Initially, Rohit was selected for his off-spin bowling. Coach Dinesh, however, noticed Rohit's batting strength when he spotted him knocking the ball with his bat. Immediately, Rohit got promoted up the batting order in his team. And, in the next season, he was selected for the Harris (Under-16) and Giles Shield tournament. The young boy could not believe his luck.

Did you know?

Rohit Sharma can speak four languages—English, Hindi, Marathi and Telugu.

Drive to Fame

Rohit's talent for the game of cricket was evident by now. In 2006, as a part of India's Under-19 cricket squad, Rohit travelled to Namibia, Scotland, Sri Lanka, the West Indies, England and Pakistan. He was now one of India's most dependable batsmen in the limited overs format. In Sri Lanka, he scored three consecutive fifties to help the country reach the finals. Rohit was clearly on the path to success.

I was amazed at the swing of the bat and the grip and started wondering where this talented batsman had cropped up from. Only when I went closer did I realise it was Rohit.

~ Dinesh Lad

Playing for India

Rohit made his international debut in an ODI match against Ireland on 23 June 2007, at Belfast. He was placed low in the batting order, at number seven. He did not get a chance to bat in that game as India won by nine wickets. It was only about five months later that he managed to make a mark when he scored his first ODI half-century (52) against arch-rivals Pakistan at Jaipur.

Rohit was later selected for the Indian squad for the 2007–08 Commonwealth Bank Series (CBS) in Australia. His fantastic flick of the wrist, among other classy shots, helped him score 235 runs, which included two half-centuries. He scored 66 runs in the first final at Sydney.

Rohit hit his first ODI century (114) on 28 May 2010, against Zimbabwe. He scored 69 runs off the last 36 balls, to score his maiden ODI century and give India a fighting total on a flat track. This was immediately followed by another century in the next match of the tri-series against Sri Lanka, when he scored 101 not out.

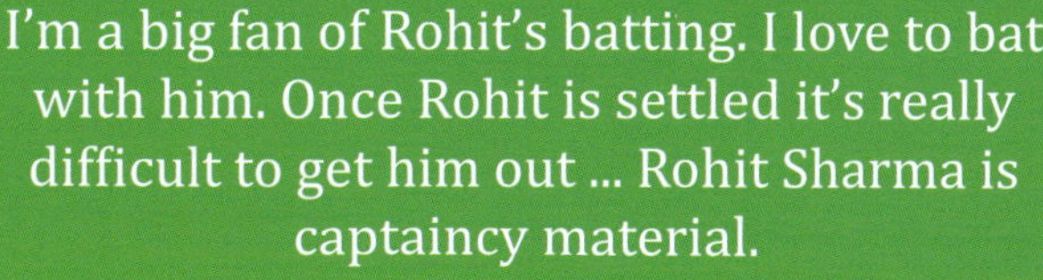

I'm a big fan of Rohit's batting. I love to bat with him. Once Rohit is settled it's really difficult to get him out ... Rohit Sharma is captaincy material.

~ Virat Kohli

'My job is to help Virat in the field. He is the captain, and whenever he looks up, I should be around.'

Winning Strokes

In November 2014, Rohit made a record 264 ODI runs in India's fourth game of the five-match series against Sri Lanka. This became the highest individual score in ODIs. He was given a special award for this by the Board of Control for Cricket in India (BCCI).

'Once you get past 100, it is all about not making a mistake.'

Very well batted, Rohit. That's Rohit for everyone—sheer talent. Enjoy and witness the class in action.

~ M.S. Dhoni

Among all the records that Rohit holds, some stand out in particular.

- He is the only batsman to score three double hundreds in ODI matches.
- He hit 16 sixes in a single match to create the record for the maximum sixes, at a match in 2013.
- He is the only batsman to have scored 10 sixes in an international match.
- He hit four consecutive sixes twice in international matches.

- Rohit has made four centuries in Twenty20 International cricket, which is the highest number of 100s hit in this format.
- He also holds the record for the fastest T20 International century. He made this 100 runs against Sri Lanka in just 35 balls. He shares the record with David Miller of South Africa.
- Finally, Rohit is the only batsman who has scored eight innings of 150-plus runs in ODIs.

His Mother's Choice

Rohit and the great Jamaican batsman, Chris Gayle, have the same jersey number 45. Since the number Rohit wanted—19—was not available, his mother insisted that he chose 45.

Other great achievements:

- Rohit was declared the ODI player of 2019 by the International Cricket Council (ICC).
- He is the first Indian to hit 400 sixes in international cricket.

'Your outer world reflects the state of your inner world. By controlling the thoughts that you think and the way you respond to the events of your life, you begin to control your destiny.'

Did you know?

Rohit once bunked school to meet his batting idol Virender Sehwag.

Sheer Class

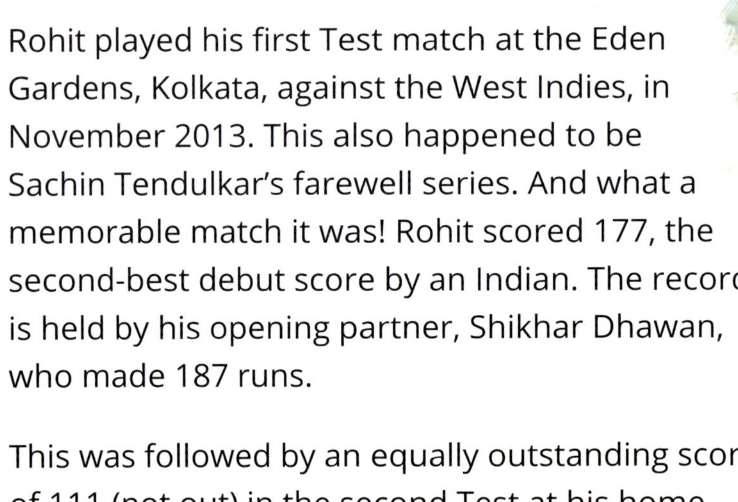

Rohit played his first Test match at the Eden Gardens, Kolkata, against the West Indies, in November 2013. This also happened to be Sachin Tendulkar's farewell series. And what a memorable match it was! Rohit scored 177, the second-best debut score by an Indian. The record is held by his opening partner, Shikhar Dhawan, who made 187 runs.

This was followed by an equally outstanding score of 111 (not out) in the second Test at his home ground—the Wankhede Stadium in Mumbai.

Rohit is a natural when it comes to the lively pitches of Australia. Not surprising, then, that the selectors decided to recall him for the tour of Australia in 2018–19, even though he had not been a part of the Test team since 2017.

The latest records reveal that though Rohit has played just 32 Test matches, he has scored 2,141 runs at an impressive average of 46.54, with one double century, six centuries and 10 half-centuries.

If Rohit can turn his white ball exploits into red ball cricket, he will be the most destructive batsman in the world after Viv Richards and Virender Sehwag.

~ Sunil Gavaskar

Did you know?

When Rohit Sharma is not hitting the ball with his bat, he is apparently losing personal belongings like his iPad, wallet, cell phone, etc. He has misplaced his passport too, a few times. The joke is that the team bus doesn't move now, till the team manager is sure that Rohit has all his things in place!

God's Gift to Cricket

Rohit had an amazing run as a part of the Ranji Trophy and India A teams, which included an unbeaten triple century at the Ranji level.

Since his debut in 2007, he had been in the Indian ODI team on and off. He made an impression in the 2007–08 CBS in Australia, playing some crucial games against stalwarts such as Brett Lee and Stuart Clark. He scored 235 runs, with an average of 33.57 with two half-centuries, in that series. However, he lost his position subsequently to Suresh Raina and then to the rising star, Virat Kohli, due to loss of form.

He's the God of one-day cricket. It's not a joke to score 200 thrice in ODIs—one can do it once, but to do it thrice is amazing.

~ Dinesh Lad

'Seeing off the new ball is important for me. I know that once I do that, the only way I can get out is from my own mistake.'

It was only in the 2013 ICC Champions Trophy that Rohit Sharma found a more secure place. His then captain M.S. Dhoni promoted him to the opening position from number seven in the batting line-up.

Did you know?

Rohit loves to sleep, and according to Virat Kohli, he sleeps the most among the members of the Indian cricket team.

All Eyes on Rohit!

As captain of the Mumbai Indians team for the Indian Premier League (IPL), Rohit has led the men in blue and gold to victory four times already. This makes him the first captain to lead his team to four IPL victories.

Rohit joined the IPL in 2008, when the Hyderabad-based Deccan Chargers signed him for US$ 750,000 a year, in a much-sought-after auction. Three years later, in the 2011 IPL player's auction, he was auctioned for US$ 2 million to the Mumbai Indians, much to their delight. As part of the Mumbai Indians team, Rohit has added several feathers to his cap.

Victory Runs in the IPL

With a total of 4,898 runs, including a century, Rohit is the third-highest run-scorer after Virat Kohli and Suresh Raina, in the T20 format. The run-getter is also among the top 10 players who have scored 4,000 runs in the IPL, as of September 2020.

Did you know?

Rohit is a very big fan of Manchester United Football Club.

A New Visitor

It was a special moment for Rohit when his daughter, Samaira, visited the cricket field for her first IPL, in 2019.

In Brilliant Form

Rohit made his World Cup debut in the 11th World Cup, in March 2015. He played eight matches for India, in the tournament held in Australia.

He was appointed vice-captain of the Indian World Cup squad in 2019. He was in top form and went on to hit five centuries. With this, Rohit became the first batsman in the tournament's history to score that many centuries in a single edition.

He was also the leading run-scorer with a huge total of 648 runs, just 25 runs short of Sachin Tendulkar's record 673 runs. He was presented the ICC's Golden Bat Award for this.

'Of course I like to watch myself bat. After every innings, match, series, I do watch my own videos whenever I get the time.'

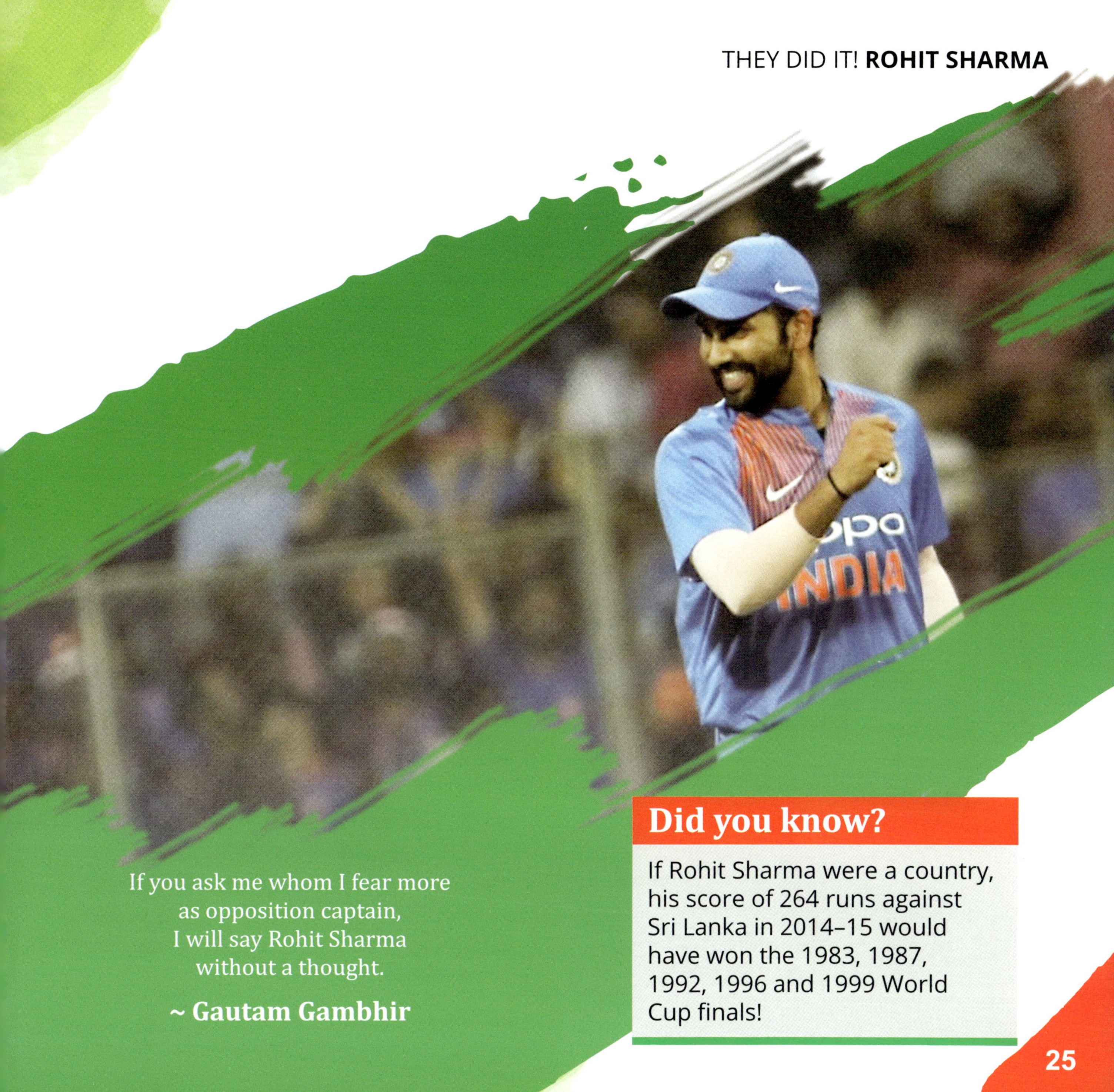

If you ask me whom I fear more
as opposition captain,
I will say Rohit Sharma
without a thought.

~ Gautam Gambhir

Did you know?

If Rohit Sharma were a country, his score of 264 runs against Sri Lanka in 2014–15 would have won the 1983, 1987, 1992, 1996 and 1999 World Cup finals!

Living Up to His Standards

Tracing cricketing journeys, it is evident that talent and luck go hand-in-hand. In Rohit's case, had Yuvraj Singh not been injured during the 2007 World T20 championship, perhaps he would not have been called upon to join the team. He might have had to wait much longer to be part of the T20 India team. In the final group stage match against South Africa, Rohit played his classic shots and stood firm under pressure. He ultimately steered India towards victory, knocking South Africa out of the tournament.

India went on to win the championship against arch-rivals Pakistan by a mere five runs!

He is probably the best T20 player I have ever seen.

~ Ricky Ponting

'I am not someone like AB de Villiers, Gayle, or Dhoni. I don't have that much power. I have to use my brain to manipulate the field and stick to my strength, which is to hit through the lines.'

In the second T20 International match against the West Indies in August 2019, in Florida, Rohit made 67 runs off 51 balls.

With this, he claimed another major T20 International record—maximum career sixes in the format.

Focusing on Performance

Rohit's superb talent as a cricketer makes him stand out from the rest. When he was asked to open the innings, Rohit felt encouraged to further hone his skills. And, once he had proved his worth, there was no stopping him. Rohit's cricketing prowess ensured a senior position for him in the team.

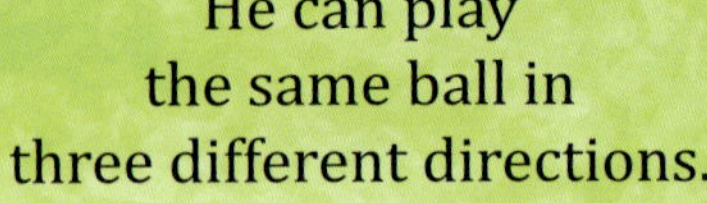

He can play
the same ball in
three different directions.

~ Sunil Gavaskar

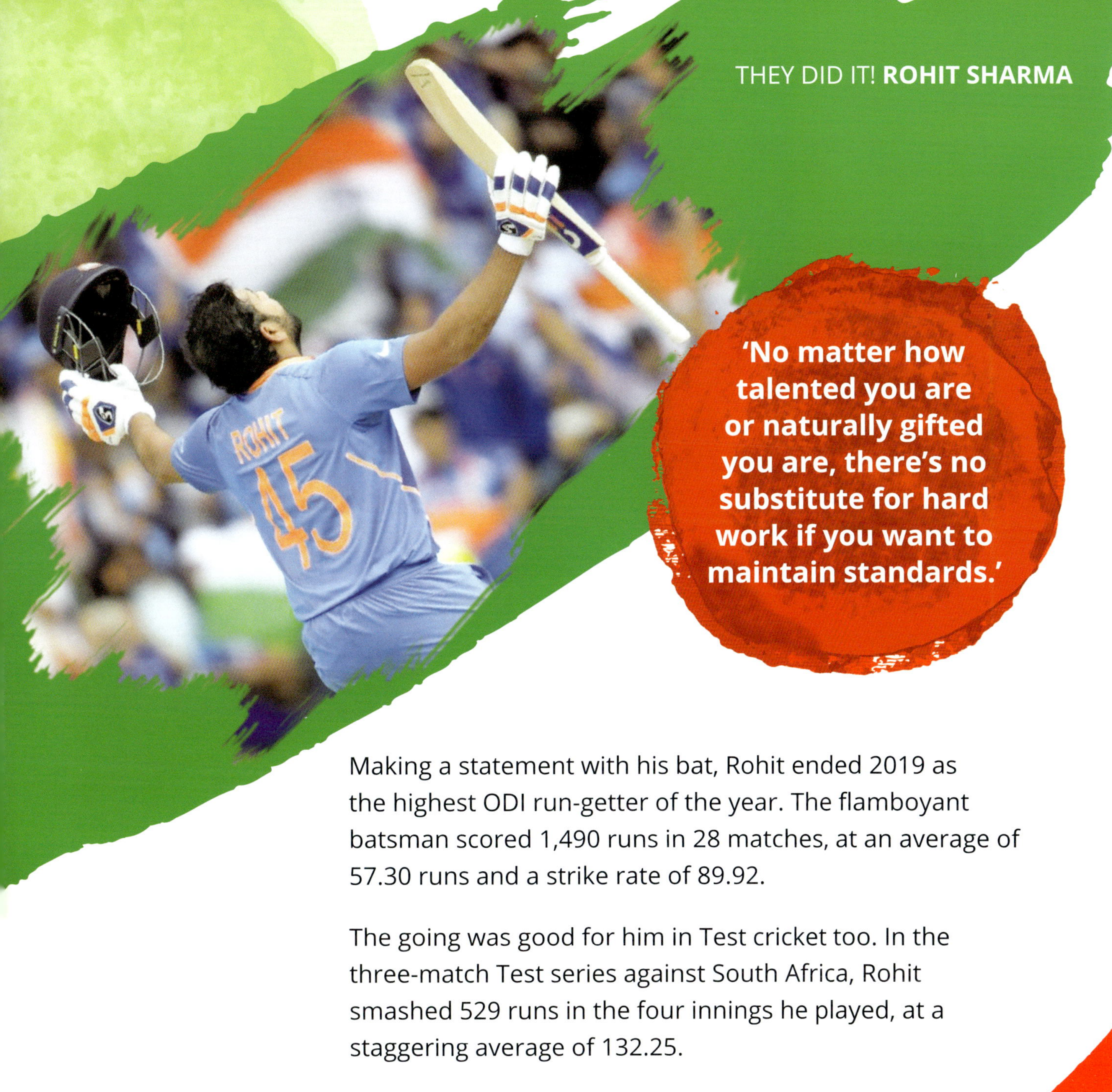

'No matter how talented you are or naturally gifted you are, there's no substitute for hard work if you want to maintain standards.'

Making a statement with his bat, Rohit ended 2019 as the highest ODI run-getter of the year. The flamboyant batsman scored 1,490 runs in 28 matches, at an average of 57.30 runs and a strike rate of 89.92.

The going was good for him in Test cricket too. In the three-match Test series against South Africa, Rohit smashed 529 runs in the four innings he played, at a staggering average of 132.25.

The Figures Speak for Themselves

2141 Runs in **32** Tests

9115 Runs in **224** ODIs

2773 Runs in **108** T20Is

7118 Runs in **92** First Class Cricket

As of 1 September 2020, Rohit has scored 39 international centuries—six in Test cricket, 29 in ODIs and four in Twenty20 Internationals. He is jointly ranked at 17th position among players with the most centuries in international cricket.

Looking Ahead

Rohit is not a regular bowler, yet he manages well when asked to bowl. His right arm off-spin bowling has often proved useful for the team. He usually fields in the slips and is trying hard to improve this aspect of his game.

Hard Work Pays

Single-minded focus and perseverance is the mantra for Rohit. His passion for cricket, along with his determination to succeed, has won him several awards.

In 2015, Rohit was honoured with the Arjuna Award by the Government of India. Besides this, he is the only player in the world to have won the ESPN Cricinfo Award for three consecutive years. He is also the only individual to score above 250 runs in ODIs, for which he was presented a special award by the BCCI in 2014.

Did you know?

As this book goes into print, the BCCI has nominated Rohit for the prestigious Khel Ratna Award 2020.

Great Innings

2019
ICC's ODI Cricketer of the Year for his 'incredible run of form' through the year

2019
ICC Cricket World Cup Golden Bat Award

2019
CEAT International ODI Cricketer of the Year

2018
Shiv Chhatrapati State Sports Award

2018
GQ Sporting Elegance

2016
CEAT Indian Cricketer of the Year

2015
GQ Sportsperson of the Year

2015
ESPN Cricinfo Award for Best T20 Innings of the Year

2014
ESPN Cricinfo Award for Best ODI Innings of the Year

2013
ESPN Cricinfo Award for Best ODI Innings of the Year

2013
Dilip Sardesai Award for Best Indian Cricketer of the Year

The Game of Love

Rohit met Ritika Sajdeh in the early days of his international cricket career. Their friendship grew over six years and finally love blossomed. In April 2015, Rohit proposed to Ritika at the Borivali Sports Club, where he had started his career. Eight months later, they were married. On 30 December 2018, they were blessed with a gorgeous baby girl, Samaira. Ritika has been interested in sports since her school days and works as a sports manager. It was cricketer Yuvraj Singh, her Rakhi brother, who introduced her to Rohit, whom she now calls 'Ro'.

'From best friends to soulmates, couldn't get any better.'

Friends Forever

A people's person, Rohit has won himself several friends, on and off the field. He has often been spotted bonding with Shikhar Dhawan, Dhawal Kulkarni, Yuzvendra Chahal and others. He also tries to keep in touch with those with whom he played cricket during his early days.

Shikhar and Rohit, in particular, share a great relationship on and off-the-field. The two opening batsmen have been friends since they played together in the Indian U-19 team. Shikhar once said in an interview, that their comfort with each other is reflected during their partnerships on the field.

Another friend, roommate and teammate, Abhishek Nayar, has played a positive role in Rohit's life. He has always stood by Rohit, and their fun times together include an incident when Rohit and his gang played a prank on the streets of Mumbai, during rush hour. Prashant Naik, another Mumbai batsman and Rohit's friend for almost two decades now, is also a part of the same group.

Rohit, reportedly, missed his friends and teammates during the lockdown due to the pandemic, and stayed in touch with them through video and phone calls.

When Rohit was not included in the 2011 World Cup squad, it was Abhishek Nayar who changed Rohit's lifestyle, getting his friend out of his comfort zone and training to get fitter.

~ Vivek Bendre

Did you know?

A friend once challenged Rohit to eat 45 eggs, which he did effortlessly.

His Favourite Things

Bollywood films, cars and vada pav are a few of Rohit's favourite things. If Govinda or Rajpal Yadav are acting in a movie, you can be sure that Rohit will watch it. And, when it comes to cars, Rohit loves making his dreams come true.

Coach Dinesh recalled how, once, while standing next to a Mercedes, eating street food, Rohit had confidently said he would own such a car one day. Not long afterwards, Rohit called Dinesh from Australia, asking him to convince his father to let him buy a BMW!

Connecting with Nature

Rohit loves animals and promotes various causes for their upkeep. In February 2015, he joined People for the Ethical Treatment of Animals (PETA), to support the sterilisation of homeless cats and dogs. In 2018, on World Rhino Day, Rohit was made the official Rhino Ambassador for WWF-India.